Simple Porridge Cookbook

Easy Delicious Porridge Recipes that Can Be Enjoyed at Any Time of Day

Table of Contents

Introduction 4

    Leek Oatmeal Porridge... 6

Vegan Porridge... 9

    Sweet Millet Congee 11

    Breakfast Porridge 13

    Overnight Apple Cranberry Steel Cut Oats 16

    Vegetable Oatmeal Porridge 19

    Buckwheat Porridge... 22

    Chicken Oatmeal Porridge..................................... 24

    Vanilla Latte Steel Cut Oats 27

    Hemp Seed Strawberry Porridge 29

    Porridge Dumplings 31

    Traditional Oatmeal Porridge............................... 34

    Slow Cooked Oatmeal Porridge........................... 37

    Dairy free Oatmeal Porridge 39

    Oat Mushroom Porridge 41

    Breakfast Quinoa 44

    Fruit Morning Porridge 46

    Oat flakes Porridge 49

    Oat Flakes Porridge with Turmeric and Dry Lime 51

    Instant Pot Cornmeal Porridge 53

    Crunchy Bacon Porridge 55

Semolina Porridge..58

Creamy Oat Flake Porridge...60

Dinner Nutritious Porridge...63

Dry Fruits Oatmeal Porridge..66

Sweet Oatmeal Porridge 69

Raisin Nut Porridge 71

Apple Porridge 73

Peanut Butter Chocolate Porridge......................................75

Plantain Porridge 77

Cornmeal Porridge 79

Conclusion 81

Introduction

If you love porridge, then this is the perfect book for you. This Simple Porridge Cookbook will expose you to 30 grain-based porridge recipes that are filled with nutrients and extremely tasty. If you are new to the world of porridges this book will serve as a simple guide to your first 30 porridge recipes. A porridge is a traditional dish commonly served as a breakfast cereal. It is usually made by boiling grains or other starchy plants in liquid (typically milk or water) with a variety of flavoring agents. The dish is typically served warm but can also be enjoyed cold. The best way to learn the depths of porridge, however, is to practice. So, lets dive into the delicious recipes to get you under way.

Leek Oatmeal Porridge

This porridge is easy to whip up and is extremely delicious.

Serves: 6

Time: 35 mins.

Ingredients:

- 8 oz leek
- 1 cup oatmeal
- 1 cup cream
- 4 cup chicken stock
- 1 teaspoon salt

- 1 teaspoon ground black pepper
- 1 bay leaf
- 1 tablespoon sour cream
- 1 teaspoon cilantro
- 3 tablespoon chives
- 4 medium potatoes, peeled
- 1 teaspoon basil

Directions:

1. Wash the leek and chop it.

2. Put the chopped leek in the big saucepan and add chicken stock.

3. Simmer such a liquid mixture on the medium heat for 10 minutes.

4. Add bay leaf.

5. Put it in the Porridge.

6. Cook the Porridge until the potato is soft.

7. Then Discard the bay leaf and make the Porridge smooth with the help of the hand blender.

8. Sprinkle the creamy Porridge with the cilantro, sour cream, basil, salt, ground black pepper, and cream.

9. Add oatmeal and churn the Porridge.

10. Close the lid and keep cooking the Porridge for 15 minutes more.

11. Then churn it gently again and remove from the heat.

12. Sprinkle the Porridge with the chives.

13. Ladle the Porridge and serve it.

14. Enjoy!

Sweet Millet Congee

A congee is much like a filling porridge, this Sweet Millet Congee leaves you feeling satisfied and filled with enough energy to carry on with your day.

Serves: 4

Time: 2 hrs. 15 mins.

Ingredients:

- Millet (1 cup, hulled, rinsed, drained)
- Water (5 cups)
- Sweet potato (1 cup, peeled, diced)

- Cinnamon (1 tsp., ground)
- Stevia (2 tbsp.)
- Apple (1 medium, diced)
- Honey (¼ cup)

Directions:

1. In a deep pot, add your stevia, sweet potato, cinnamon, water, and millet then stir to combine.

2. Allow to boil on high heat then switch to low to reduce to a simmer.

3. Cook like this for about an hour, on until your water is fully absorbed and millet is cooked.

4. Stir in your remaining Ingredients and serve.

Breakfast Porridge

This porridge is both savory and sweet, making it the perfect start to any day.

Serves: 9

Time: 35 min

Ingredients:

- 1 cup green beans
- ½ cup sweet corn
- 1 tablespoon paprika

- 1 teaspoon salt
- 2 cups oatmeal
- ½ cup rice
- 1 cup milk
- 8 cups chicken stock
- 1 carrot
- 3 oz shallot
- 5 medium potatoes
- 1 teaspoon ground white pepper
- 1 teaspoon oregano
- ¼ teaspoon ground coriander

Directions:

1. Combine the chicken stock and rice in the vessel.

2. Sprinkle the liquid with the oregano, ground black pepper, and ground white pepper.

3. Close the lid and start to cook the Porridge.

4. Meanwhile, chop the shallot and peel the carrot.

5. Cut the carrot into the cubes.

6. Add the chopped shallot and carrot cubes to the Porridge mixture.

7. Peel potatoes and cut them into the medium cubes. Add the potato in the Porridge.

8. Then add milk and oatmeal.

9. Sprinkle the Porridge with the paprika and salt.

10. Cook the Porridge on the medium heat for 5 minutes and add sweet corn and green beans.

11. Cook the Porridge for 10 minutes more or till it cooked.

12. When the Porridge is ready to eat, ladle it into the serving bowls.

13. Serve the dish immediately.

14. Enjoy!

Overnight Apple Cranberry Steel Cut Oats

Overnight oatmeal porridge is a common way to start a busy day and now you can enjoy it as well with this recipe.

Serves: 6

Time: 50 mins.

Ingredients:

- Oats (2 cups, steel cut)
- Milk (2 cups)
- Yogurt (1 cup)
- Water (3 cup)
- Apples (4, diced)
- Cranberries (1½ cup, fresh)
- Coconut oil (2 tbsp.)
- Lemon juice (1 tsp., fresh)
- Cinnamon (2 tsp.)
- Nutmeg (½ tsp.)
- Maple syrup (¼ cup)
- Salt (½ tsp.)
- 2 tsp. vanilla (optional)

Directions:

1. Fit your steel basket insert into your Instant Pot and use oil to lightly grease the bottom of the insert.

2. Add in all your Ingredients, except vanilla, maple syrup, and salt then allow to sit overnight.

3. When you are ready to cook in the morning simply stir and set your Instant Pot to manual with a 7 minutes timer.

4. It may take up 20 minutes to get to high pressure. After your timer goes off, press cancel, and allow the cooker to cool naturally for about 10 minutes.

5. When done, release the pressure naturally (should take about 10 minutes).

6. Once cooled, add in your remaining Ingredients and stir to combine. Enjoy!

Vegetable Oatmeal Porridge

Get your portions of veggies in this simple Vegetable Oatmeal Porridge.

Serves: 10

Time: 40 mins.

Ingredients:

- 3 cups oatmeal
- ½ cup fresh dill

- 1 teaspoon chili flakes
- 1 medium sweet pepper
- 1 zucchini
- 1 teaspoon ground black pepper
- ½ tablespoon salt
- 5 oz cauliflower
- 9 cups water

Directions:

1. Peel the zucchini and wash the cauliflower.

2. Chop the vegetables into the available pieces and place them in the saucepan.

3. Add water and start to cook the Porridge.

4. After 10 minutes add the ground black pepper, salt, and chili flakes.

5. Then chop the sweet pepper and dill.

6. Add the chopped sweet pepper and fresh dill to the Porridge and simmer it for 5 minutes more.

7. Then add oatmeal and close the lid.

8. Cook the Porridge for 10 minutes more on the medium heat.

9. Then open the lid and check if all the vegetables and the oatmeal cooked.

10. Discard the Porridge from the heat and leave it for 10 minutes.

11. After this, ladle the Porridge into the serving bowls.

12. Serve it hot or warm.

13. Enjoy!

Buckwheat Porridge

This tasty porridge can be whipped up in under an hour and enjoyed as breakfast or lunch.

Serves: 4

Time: 30 mins.

Ingredients:

- Buckwheat groats (1 cup, raw, rinsed)
- Rice milk (3 cups)
- Banana (1, sliced)

- Raisins (1/4 cup)
- Cinnamon (1 tsp., ground)
- Vanilla (1/2 tsp.)
- Nuts (1/2 cup, chopped)

Directions:

1. Fit your steel basket into your Instant Pot. Add all your Ingredients to the pot and set to pressure on high with your timer set to 6 minutes.

2. When done, allow your cooker to cool down naturally for about 20 minutes before attempting to open.

3. Carefully open the lid, top with nuts, and serve. Enjoy!

Chicken Oatmeal Porridge

If you want a more savory bite, enjoy this tasty Chicken Oatmeal Porridge.

Serves: 11

Time: 45 mins.

Ingredients:

- 1-pound chicken breast
- 3 medium potatoes, peeled, cubed
- 2 carrots
- 3 oz shallot
- 1 yellow onion

- 2 cup oatmeal
- 3 tablespoon cream
- 8 cups water
- 1 tablespoon salt
- 1 teaspoon ground white pepper
- 1 teaspoon oregano
- 1 teaspoon cilantro
- ¼ cup fresh dill
- ½ cup milk
- 2 tablespoon chives

Directions:

1. Chop the chicken breast roughly and put it in the big saucepan.

2. Add water and start to cook the chicken stock.

3. Sprinkle the meat with the salt and ground white pepper.

4. Add oregano and cilantro.

5. When the mixture is about to boil, discard the foam from the surface.

6. Peel the carrots and cut them into the cubes.

7. After this, add the vegetables in the chicken stock and continue to cook it.

8. Chop the chives and shallot.

9. Peel the onion and dice it.

10. Add the chopped chives and shallot in the Porridge.

11. After this, add the diced onion.

12. When all the vegetables are half cooked – add the oatmeal and milk.

13. Close the lid and cook the Porridge for 10 minutes more.

14. Add the cream at the end of the cooking and simmer the Porridge for 5 minutes more.

15. When the Porridge cooked – remove it from the heat and let it rest for several minutes. Enjoy!

Vanilla Latte Steel Cut Oats

This delicious oatmeal porridge is laced with vanilla and can be whipped up in minutes.

Serves 4

Time: 25 mins.

Ingredients:

- Water (2 1/2 cup)
- Whole Milk (1 cup)
- Oats (1 cup, steel cut, dry)
- Sugar (2 tbsp. granulated)

- Cocoa powder (1 tsp., unsweetened)
- Salt (1/4 tsp)
- Vanilla (2 tsp., extract)
- Whipped cream topping (1 tbsp.)

Directions:

1. Fit your steel basket insert into your Instant Pot. Add in all your Ingredients, except vanilla, whipped cream, and chocolate, and stir well to combine.

2. Set your Instant Pot to pressure on high with a 10 minutes timer. After your timer goes off, press cancel, and allow the cooker to cool naturally for about 10 minutes.

3. When done, release the pressure naturally (may take about 10 minutes).

4. Once cooled, add in your remaining Ingredients and stir to combine. Enjoy!

Hemp Seed Strawberry Porridge

This delicious porridge is creamy, tasty and can be whipped up in minutes.

Serves: 4

Time: 20 mins.

Ingredients:

- 400 - 500 g of oatmeal with hemp seeds
- 250 – 300 g of hot water
- 250 g of cheese cream
- 100 g of powdered sugar (vanilla flavor preferred)

- 400 – 500 g of strawberries
- Peeled hemp seeds
- Almond flakes (for decoration only)

Directions:

1. Put the cheese cream and the powdered sugar in a bowl and mix them.

2. Add the oatmeal with hemp seeds (save a tablespoon of powdered sugar for later).

3. Gradually add in your hot water then mix constantly. The mix must not be too thin therefore we must pour the hot water slowly.

4. In an ice, cream cup puts 2 – 3 tablespoons of the resulted porridge and add a few half-sliced strawberries on top.

5. Add 2 – 3 tablespoons of cheese cream.

6. Put another layer of sliced strawberries, then another layer of porridge.

7. Last step: add on top a fine strawberry and scatter peeled hemp seeds and almond flakes. Enjoy!

Porridge Dumplings

This savory porridge is hassle free and delicious.

Serves: 6

Time: 60 mins.

Ingredients:

- 2 l water
- 1 parsley root
- 1 celery
- 3 threads green onion
- 2 tablespoons olive oil
- 2 eggs
- 1 tablespoon cheese (cow)
- 6 tablespoons oatmeal
- Grinded salt and pepper
- Green parsley

Directions:

1. Stir the eggs thoroughly; add cheese, oatmeal, a little salt, and pepper. Put the mixture aside to blend properly.

2. Slice thinly parsley root, celery and green onion and put them in a pot to boil in water.

3. When the chopped vegetables boiled, use a small spoon to add small pieces of the mixture (dumplings) resulted in step 1.

4. Wait until the dumplings surface then pour a pot of cold water.

5. It is important to add SMALL dumplings as they grow considerably when boiled in water

6. Keep the pot at low heat until the dumplings are boiled.

7. Season with salt and pepper to taste, turn off the heat and add the green parsley chopped into small pieces.

8. To be served warm.

Traditional Oatmeal Porridge

If you love the classics, then this porridge is perfect for you.

Serves: 7

Time: 40 mins.

Ingredients:

- 3 onions
- 5 cups chicken stock
- 1 tablespoon salt

- 1 tablespoon sour cream
- 3 tablespoon scallion
- 1 teaspoon chili flakes
- 1 tablespoon dill
- 1 tablespoon butter
- 2 cups oatmeal
- 1 carrot
- 1 sweet green pepper
- 1 tablespoon olive oil

Directions:

1. Peel the onions and dice them.

2. Then put the diced onion in the pan and sprinkle it with the olive oil.

3. Simmer the onions for 10 minutes on the medium heat.

4. Meanwhile, pour the chicken stock into the big saucepan and add salt.

5. After this, add the oatmeal and start to cook it.

6. Peel the carrot and grate it.

7. Add the grated carrot in the oatmeal mixture.

8. Then add the cooked diced onion.

9. Sprinkle the Porridge liquid with the dill, chili flakes, and scallion.

10. Chop the sweet green pepper into the small pieces and add to the Porridge.

11. When all the ingredients of the Porridge cooked – blend it with the help of the hand blender.

12. Add the dill and scallions to the blended Porridge.

13. Then add sour cream and churn it with the help of the wooden spoon.

14. Add butter and leave the Porridge for 10 minutes to rest.

15. Ladle the cooked Porridge in the bowls.

16. Enjoy!

Slow Cooked Oatmeal Porridge

This recipe will give you the most favour-oriented bowl of oatmeal you have ever had.

Serves: 8

Time: 9 hrs. 6 mins.

Ingredients:

- Fat-free milk (4 cups)
- Water (4 cups)
- Steel-cut oats (2 cups)
- Cup raisins (1/3 cup)

- Dried cherries (1/3 cup)
- Dried apricots (1/3 cup, chopped)
- Molasses (1 tsp.)
- Cinnamon (1 tsp.)
- Nutmeg (1/2 tsp.)

Directions:

1. Combine all ingredients in a slow cooker. Turn on low heat.

2. Seal lid, cook for 8 to 9 hours overnight.

3. Ladle into bowls. Serve.

Dairy free Oatmeal Porridge

Here is a porridge that you can enjoy when lactose free diets.

Serves: 4

Time: 20 mins.

Ingredients:

- 1 cup soy milk
- 2 cups water
- 1 teaspoon turmeric
- 1/3 teaspoon cinnamon

- ¼ cup almond milk
- 3 cups oatmeal
- 2 tablespoon stevia
- 1 teaspoon vanilla extract

Directions:

1. Preheat the water in the saucepan and then add soy milk.

2. Mix up the liquid carefully and add almond milk.

3. After this, sprinkle the juice with the oatmeal and stir it thoroughly.

4. Then add cinnamon and vanilla extract.

5. Close the saucepan and lid and simmer the dish for 8 minutes. Stir it time to time.

6. When the porridge is cooked, chill it little and add stevia.

7. Then transfer the cooked oatmeal into the serving bowls and sprinkle the dish with the turmeric.

8. Serve the baked oatmeal only hot or warm.

9. Enjoy!

Oat Mushroom Porridge

If you have the time to dedicate a bowl of deliciousness, then this porridge was a must try.

Serves: 4 – 5

Time: 60 mins.

Ingredients:

- 1 onion
- 2 carrots
- 1 parsley root
- 2 celery roots
- 150g fresh mushrooms
- 40 g butter
- 50 g oat flakes
- 2 L water
- Salt and pepper
- Celery leaves (for decoration)

Directions:

1. Peel and wash onion, carrots, parsley roots and 1 celery root. Chop the carrots and parsley root in half, then into slim slices.

2. Wash the mushrooms thoroughly and slice them thin pieces. The onion must be thinly chopped and a celery root in thin round slices.

3. Put the butter in a pot and let it melt. Add the onion, carrots, parsley root, round slices of celery and fry them till soften.

4. Add the oat flakes, pour water and stir. Keep on the stove until vegetables are boiled, around 15 minutes.

5. Toss in the sliced mushrooms and keep boiling for 10 more minutes.

6. Chop the 1 celery root left into thin long slices, add it to the mixture and boil for 10 more minutes.

7. Adjust the seasoning, garnish with celery leaves, and enjoy.

Breakfast Quinoa

If you love quinoa this quinoa porridge will be your undoing.

Serves: 6 Servings

Time: 26 Minutes

Ingredients:

For Quinoa:

- Quinoa (1 1/2 cups, uncooked, well-rinsed)
- Water (2 1/4 cups)
- Maple syrup (2 tbsp.)

Ingredients:

- ½ cup blueberry
- 2 bananas
- 1 cup strawberry
- 3 cups oatmeal
- 4 cups milk
- ½ cup blackberry
- 3 tablespoon honey
- 1 teaspoon sugar
- 2 tablespoon water
- 1 tablespoon butter

Directions:

1. Combine the oatmeal and milk in the big saucepan and close the lid.

2. Put the mixture in the oven and cook it on the medium heat for 15 minutes.

3. Then add the butter and poach it gently.

4. Close the lid and leave the dish for 10 minutes to relax.

5. Meanwhile, wash the blueberries, strawberries, and blackberries.

6. Place the fruits in the pan and add water.

7. After this, add sugar and simmer the benefits for 5 minutes on the medium heat.

8. When the fruits cooked – remove them from the heat and discard from the liquid.

9. Then peel the bananas and slice them.

10. Put the cooked porridge in the serving bowls and add honey. Mix it up.

11. Then sprinkle the cooked dish with the cooked fruits and sliced bananas.

12. Enjoy!

Oat flakes Porridge

This tasty porridge is amazingly easy to cook and makes for a tasty breakfast on the go.

Serves: 4

Time: 15 mins.

Ingredients:

- 1 l water
- 4 tablespoons oat flakes
- 1 carrot
- 1 tablespoon margarine

- 1 egg
- 1/2 bundle green parsley, sliced
- Mixed vegetable seasonings, chopped

Directions:

1. Add your vegetables into a medium saucepan.

2. Add the margarine and let them boil at low heat until the vegetables soften. Add water.

3. Add the carrot chopped in round slices and season with mixed vegetables to taste.

4. Boil for 6 – 7 more minutes. Also, boil the egg and chop it thinly.

5. After the mixture boiled, stir in the chopped egg and scatter thinly sliced green parsley. Enjoy!

Oat Flakes Porridge with Turmeric and Dry Lime

This Indian inspired porridge is spicy and delicious.

Serves: 4

Time: 40 mins.

Ingredients:

- 1 l water
- 1 onion, chopped

- 1 carrot, chopped
- 1 tablespoon turmeric
- 1 potato, peeled and cubed
- 1 tablespoon tomato paste
- 1 tablespoon exotic seasoning mix
- 1 dry lime, green parsley
- 50 g oat flakes

Directions:

1. Set your water on to boil. Add your seasonings, tomato paste, turmeric, carrot and onion.

2. Break the dry lime to release flavor and add it to the mixture.

3. Let it boil for 10 more minutes then stir in the potato cubes and the oat flakes.

4. Allow to boil for another 10 minutes then remove the dry lime (not to be eaten).

5. Scatter with thinly chopped green parsley and exotic seasoning mix. Enjoy!

Instant Pot Cornmeal Porridge

Now you can enjoy tasty cornmeal porridge in minutes from your instant pot using this hassle free recipe.

Serves: 4

Time: 30 mins.

Ingredients:

- Cornmeal (1 cup)
- Rice milk (3 cups)
- Banana (1, sliced)
- Raisins (1/4 cup)
- Cinnamon (1 tsp., ground)

- Nutmeg (1 tsp., ground)
- Vanilla (1/2 tsp.)
- Nuts (1/2 cup, chopped)

Directions:

1. Fit your steel basket into your Instant Pot. Add all your ingredients to the pot and set to pressure on high with your timer set to 6 minutes.

2. When done, allow your cooker to cool down naturally for about 20 minutes before attempting to open.

3. Carefully open the lid, top with nuts, and serve. Enjoy!

Crunchy Bacon Porridge

Bacon makes everything better and the same can be said for this tasty porridge.

Serves: 6

Time: 35 mins.

Ingredients:

- 7 oz bacon slices
- 1/ cup almond flakes
- ¼ cup red beans, cooked
- 1 yellow onion

- 3 cups oatmeal
- 3 cups water
- 1 teaspoon salt
- 1 teaspoon cilantro
- 1 teaspoon oregano
- 1 teaspoon dried dill
- 1 tablespoon sesame seeds oil
- 1 tablespoon sesame seeds
- 2 tablespoon butter
- 1 tablespoon bread crumbs

Directions:

1. Chop the sliced bacon into the tiny pieces and sprinkle it with the cilantro and oregano.

2. Then sprinkle the chopped bacon with the sesame oil and place it in the pan.

3. Roast the bacon till it is crunchy.

4. Then remove the cooked bacon from the pan.

5. Peel the onion and chop it.

6. Put the chopped onion in the pan and fry it for 2 minutes on the medium heat.

7. Then add the cooked chopped bacon, butter, sesame seeds, sesame oil, dried dill, oregano, cilantro, and red beans.

8. Poach the mixture and simmer it on the low heat for 1 minute with the closed lid.

9. Combine the oatmeal with the water in the big saucepan and cook it with the closed lid for 15 min.

10. When the oatmeal cooked – mix it with the almond flakes and poach gently.

11. Then put the cooked oatmeal porridge in the serving bowls and add the chopped bacon mixture.

12. Serve the dish hot.

13. Enjoy!

Semolina Porridge

This tasty Semolina Porridge is the perfect way to start a cold winter day.

Serves: 4 Servings

Time: 30 Minutes

Ingredients:

- Semolina (1 cup)
- Almond milk (3 cups)

- Banana (1, sliced)
- Raisins (1/4 cup)
- Cinnamon (1 tsp., ground)
- Vanilla (1/2 tsp.)
- Almonds (1/2 cup, chopped)

Directions:

1. Fit your steel basket into your Instant Pot. Add all your ingredients to the pot and set to pressure on high with your timer set to 6 minutes.

2. When done, allow your cooker to cool down naturally for about 20 minutes before attempting to open.

3. Carefully open the lid, top with nuts, and serve. Enjoy!

Creamy Oat Flake Porridge

This creamy oat flake porridge is tasty, savory, and filing.

Serves: 10

Time: 2 hrs.

Ingredients:

- 2 carrots
- 1 root parsley
- 1 parsnip
- 1/2 celery
- 2 potatoes

- 1/4 white cabbage
- 1 egg
- 200 ml milk
- 5 tablespoons oat flakes
- 50 g margarine
- Salt, 1/2 green parsley
- 2L water

Directions:

1. Wash and clean all vegetables, put them in a pot and boil them in water with little salt.

2. After boiled, shred all vegetables in a blender with ½ cup of the boiling water.

3. Stir the ground vegetables in the boiling water and again boil on the stove.

4. When reached the boiling point, scatter the oat flakes and mix. After 5 minutes pour the hot milk and let it boil for 10 more minutes.

5. Season with the salt, and turn off the heat and add the egg mixed as in omelet.

6. Add slices of margarine on top and then scatter the parsley chopped into small pieces.

7. Cover the pot for 10 – 15 minutes, meanwhile the oat flakes will soften. Enjoy!

Dinner Nutritious Porridge

This tasty dinner porridge is delicious and extremely easy to prepare.

Serves: 5

Time: 30 mins.

Ingredients:

- 8 oz turkey fillet
- 1 teaspoon salt
- 1 teaspoon ground black pepper

- 1 tablespoon olive oil
- 1 teaspoon butter
- 2 cups oatmeal
- 1/3 cup white beans, cooked
- 1 white onion
- 1 teaspoon sugar
- ½ teaspoon cilantro
- ½ teaspoon oregano
- ½ cup cream
- 3 cups water

Directions:

1. Chop the turkey fillet into the small cubes.

2. Then sprinkle the meat with the salt and ground black pepper.

3. Mix up the mixture.

4. Pour the olive oil in the pan and preheat it well.

5. Toss the turkey cubes in the hot oil and roast it for 10 minutes on the medium heat. Stir it frequently.

6. Then add cooked white beans.

7. Peel the onion and dice it.

8. Add the diced onion to the meat mixture.

9. Pour the water into the saucepan and cook it on the high heat till it becomes to boil.

10. Then add the oatmeal and cook the porridge with the closed lid for 10 minutes. Do not worry if the oatmeal does not soak all the liquid.

11. Transfer the cooked oatmeal into the pan with the turkey mixture and stir it well.

12. Then add cream.

13. Sprinkle the mass with the oregano, cilantro, sugar, and butter.

14. Churn it well with the help of the wooden spatula and simmer with the closed lid till the components cooked.

15. Serve the dinner nutritious porridge only hot.

16. Enjoy!

Dry Fruits Oatmeal Porridge

The dry fruits make this porridge naturally sweet and tasty.

Serves: 4

Time: 15 mins.

Ingredients:

- 1 cup water
- 1 cup milk
- 2 cups oatmeal

- ¼ cup raisins
- 4 tablespoon prunes
- 1 tablespoon sugar
- ½ teaspoon salt
- 1 teaspoon ground cardamom
- 1 teaspoon cinnamon
- ¼ cup walnuts
- 1 tablespoon butter, unsalted

Directions:

1. Combine the water and milk in the big saucepan and start to preheat it on the medium heat.

2. Add sugar and salt.

3. Once boiling, add in your oatmeal and reduce the heat.

4. Cook the porridge on the medium heat for 6 minutes. Stir the porridge constantly to avoid the scorching.

5. Meanwhile, chop the prunes.

6. Then cut the raisins into the halves.

7. Crush the walnuts.

8. When the porridge cooked – sprinkle it with the cinnamon and ground cardamom.

9. Add the crushed walnuts, chopped prunes, and raisins.

10. After this, add unsalted butter.

11. Stir the porridge with the help of the spoon gently.

12. Serve it warm.

Sweet Oatmeal Porridge

This porridge is sweet, crunchy and delish.

Serves: 1

Time: 10 mins.

Ingredients:

- 50g of oatmeal
- 350ml of milk
- 1 tablespoon of sugar

- 1/4 tablespoon of salt
- Jam, fruits, nuts and honey (optional – for serving only)

Directions:

1. Put the milk, oatmeal, salt and sugar, all together in a pot.

2. Boil them, constantly mixing, at medium heat, for 5 minutes.

3. Reduce the heat to minimum and keep mixing constantly for another 5 - 7 minutes until the oatmeal is soft and the milk has become sticky.

4. Check to see if the oatmeal is properly boiled. Do not forget that the mixture will harden after cooling.

5. Pour the compound in a plate and let it cool a bit.

6. To be served with jams, fruits syrups, honey, fruits, and nuts.

Raisin Nut Porridge

This nutty porridge is tasty and filled with texture.

Serves: 1

Time: 10 mins.

Ingredients:

- 150 g of oatmeal
- 50 g of raisins
- 600 ml of water
- 50 g of grinded nuts

- 1 tablespoon of orange peel
- 50 g of sugar (or honey) cinnamon

Directions:

1. Put the water in a pot and let it boil.

2. Put the raisins in a bowl, pour the boiled water and add the oatmeal.

3. Mix everything and add the orange peel, the grinded nuts, and the sugar and keep mixing.

4. If you do not tolerate sugar then honey is the perfect substitute.

5. Sprinkle the cinnamon on top.

6. To be served warm or cooled, as wished.

Apple Porridge

Spin your apples into a tasty bowl of porridge with this hassle-free porridge.

Serves: 4

Time: 15 mins.

Ingredients:

- 400 ml of milk
- 2 apples
- 150 g of oatmeal
- 400 ml of apple juice
- 1/2 tablespoon of cinnamon
- 50 g of sugar

- 70 ml of whipped cream (preferred 10% fat)

Directions:

1. Put the oatmeal in a pot/pan then add the apple juice, the milk, and the sugar.

2. Let the compound boil but mix it constantly until it reaches the boiling point.

3. Keep boiling further for 5 more minutes, at low heat.

4. Remove the recipient from the stove and keep it covered for 5 more minutes.

5. In the meantime, wash the apples, peel them off and slice them thinly.

6. Add the thinly sliced apples to the hot porridge, together with the cinnamon and the whipped cream.

7. Mix everything properly and enjoy!

Plantain Porridge

This delicious porridge is an island porridge that serves as a common breakfast dish.

Serves: 1

Time: 20 mins.

Ingredients:

- 2 green plantains
- ½ cup coconut milk
- 1 tablespoon cinnamon

- 1 teaspoon vanilla
- 1 teaspoon nutmeg
- 3 ½ cups water
- ½ cup oats
- 1/3 cup sugar

Directions:

1. Wash and peel green plantains. Cut horizontally into 1"pieces. Add the plantains and 1 cup of water to a blender or food processor. Blend for 1 minute. Add oats and blend until smooth.

2. Add the remaining 2 cups of the water to a pot. Heat water to boil on high heat for 2 minutes.

3. Add the plantain-oats mixture to the pot. Lower the heat to medium-high temperature. Cook for 15 minutes, stirring in between.

4. Add coconut milk, nutmeg, sugar, cinnamon, and vanilla. Stir. Allow to cool for a few minutes. Top with favorite fruits or granola. Serve.

Cornmeal Porridge

This recipe produces a rich, filling and tasty porridge.

Serves: 2

Time: 30 mins.

Ingredients:

- ¼ cup cornmeal
- 2 cups water

- ¼ tsp. salt
- 4 tbsp. sugar
- ½ cup coconut milk
- 1 tsp. vanilla
- 1 tablespoon cinnamon

Directions:

1. Mix cornmeal with a little of the water.

2. Add Bring the remainder of the water to a boil and add the cornmeal and salt.

3. Continue cooking for 10 minutes.

4. Stir in coconut milk.

5. Add vanilla and cinnamon. Sweeten to taste.

Conclusion

Congrats on cooking your way through all 30 delicious porridge recipes that can all be enjoyed at anybody looking to enjoy porridges fresh from home. The next step from here would be to continue practicing. With every single porridge recipe, you create you will see magic being created as you go through this book. After you have accomplished that, come on back over and find another amazing journey to partake in from cuisines across the globe in another one of our books. We hope to see you again soon. Happy cooking!

Printed in Great Britain
by Amazon